"There's so much to see!"

Disney

Tim Burton's
THE
NIGHTMARE
BEFORE
CHRISTMAS

Danilo
WWW.DANILO.COM

Published by Danilo Promotions Ltd. Unit 3, The io Centre, Lea Road, Waltham Abbey, EN9 1AS, England.
Enquiries: **info@danilo.com** For all other information: **www.danilo.com**

Printed in China.

PERSONAL INFORMATION

NAME: _____

ADDRESS: _____

_____

MOBILE: _____

EMAIL: _____

IN CASE OF EMERGENCY PLEASE CONTACT

NAME: _____

ADDRESS: _____

_____

MOBILE: _____

DOCTOR: _____

DOCTOR TELEPHONE: _____

KNOWN ALLERGIES: _____

_____

_____

_____

_____

NOTES

JANUARY

WK	M	T	W	T	F	S	S
1	1	2	3	4	5	6	7
2	8	9	10	11	12	13	14
3	15	16	17	18	19	20	21
4	22	23	24	25	26	27	28
5	29	30	31				

FEBRUARY

WK	M	T	W	T	F	S	S
5				1	2	3	4
6	5	6	7	8	9	10	11
7	12	13	14	15	16	17	18
8	19	20	21	22	23	24	25
9	26	27	28	29			

MARCH

WK	M	T	W	T	F	S	S
9					1	2	3
10	4	5	6	7	8	9	10
11	11	12	13	14	15	16	17
12	18	19	20	21	22	23	24
13	25	26	27	28	29	30	31

APRIL

WK	M	T	W	T	F	S	S
14	1	2	3	4	5	6	7
15	8	9	10	11	12	13	14
16	15	16	17	18	19	20	21
17	22	23	24	25	26	27	28
18	29	30					

MAY

WK	M	T	W	T	F	S	S
18			1	2	3	4	5
19	6	7	8	9	10	11	12
20	13	14	15	16	17	18	19
21	20	21	22	23	24	25	26
22	27	28	29	30	31		

JUNE

WK	M	T	W	T	F	S	S
22						1	2
23	3	4	5	6	7	8	9
24	10	11	12	13	14	15	16
25	17	18	19	20	21	22	23
26	24	25	26	27	28	29	30

JULY

WK	M	T	W	T	F	S	S
27	1	2	3	4	5	6	7
28	8	9	10	11	12	13	14
29	15	16	17	18	19	20	21
30	22	23	24	25	26	27	28
31	29	30	31				

AUGUST

WK	M	T	W	T	F	S	S
31				1	2	3	4
32	5	6	7	8	9	10	11
33	12	13	14	15	16	17	18
34	19	20	21	22	23	24	25
35	26	27	28	29	30	31	

SEPTEMBER

WK	M	T	W	T	F	S	S
35							1
36	2	3	4	5	6	7	8
37	9	10	11	12	13	14	15
38	16	17	18	19	20	21	22
39	23	24	25	26	27	28	29
40	30						

OCTOBER

WK	M	T	W	T	F	S	S
40		1	2	3	4	5	6
41	7	8	9	10	11	12	13
42	14	15	16	17	18	19	20
43	21	22	23	24	25	26	27
44	28	29	30	31			

NOVEMBER

WK	M	T	W	T	F	S	S
44					1	2	3
45	4	5	6	7	8	9	10
46	11	12	13	14	15	16	17
47	18	19	20	21	22	23	24
48	25	26	27	28	29	30	

DECEMBER

WK	M	T	W	T	F	S	S
48							1
49	2	3	4	5	6	7	8
50	9	10	11	12	13	14	15
51	16	17	18	19	20	21	22
52	23	24	25	26	27	28	29
1	30	31					

JANUARY

WK	M	T	W	T	F	S	S
1			1	2	3	4	5
2	6	7	8	9	10	11	12
3	13	14	15	16	17	18	19
4	20	21	22	23	24	25	26
5	27	28	29	30	31		

FEBRUARY

WK	M	T	W	T	F	S	S
5						1	2
6	3	4	5	6	7	8	9
7	10	11	12	13	14	15	16
8	17	18	19	20	21	22	23
9	24	25	26	27	28		

MARCH

WK	M	T	W	T	F	S	S
9						1	2
10	3	4	5	6	7	8	9
11	10	11	12	13	14	15	16
12	17	18	19	20	21	22	23
13	24	25	26	27	28	29	30
14	31						

APRIL

WK	M	T	W	T	F	S	S
14		1	2	3	4	5	6
15	7	8	9	10	11	12	13
16	14	15	16	17	18	19	20
17	21	22	23	24	25	26	27
18	28	29	30				

MAY

WK	M	T	W	T	F	S	S
18				1	2	3	4
19	5	6	7	8	9	10	11
20	12	13	14	15	16	17	18
21	19	20	21	22	23	24	25
22	26	27	28	29	30	31	

JUNE

WK	M	T	W	T	F	S	S
22							1
23	2	3	4	5	6	7	8
24	9	10	11	12	13	14	15
25	16	17	18	19	20	21	22
26	23	24	25	26	27	28	29
27	30						

JULY

WK	M	T	W	T	F	S	S
27		1	2	3	4	5	6
28	7	8	9	10	11	12	13
29	14	15	16	17	18	19	20
30	21	22	23	24	25	26	27
31	28	29	30	31			

AUGUST

WK	M	T	W	T	F	S	S
31					1	2	3
32	4	5	6	7	8	9	10
33	11	12	13	14	15	16	17
34	18	19	20	21	22	23	24
35	25	26	27	28	29	30	31

SEPTEMBER

WK	M	T	W	T	F	S	S
36	1	2	3	4	5	6	7
37	8	9	10	11	12	13	14
38	15	16	17	18	19	20	21
39	22	23	24	25	26	27	28
40	29	30					

OCTOBER

WK	M	T	W	T	F	S	S
40			1	2	3	4	5
41	6	7	8	9	10	11	12
42	13	14	15	16	17	18	19
43	20	21	22	23	24	25	26
44	27	28	29	30	31		

NOVEMBER

WK	M	T	W	T	F	S	S
44						1	2
45	3	4	5	6	7	8	9
46	10	11	12	13	14	15	16
47	17	18	19	20	21	22	23
48	24	25	26	27	28	29	30

DECEMBER

WK	M	T	W	T	F	S	S
49	1	2	3	4	5	6	7
50	8	9	10	11	12	13	14
51	15	16	17	18	19	20	21
52	22	23	24	25	26	27	28
1	29	30	31				

NEW YEAR'S DAY	JAN 1
NEW YEAR HOLIDAY (SCOTLAND)	JAN 2
CHINESE NEW YEAR (DRAGON)	FEB 10
SHROVE TUESDAY	FEB 13
VALENTINE'S DAY	FEB 14
ST. DAVID'S DAY	MAR 1
INTERNATIONAL WOMEN'S DAY	MAR 8
MOTHER'S DAY (UK) & RAMADAN BEGINS	MAR 10
ST. PATRICK'S DAY	MAR 17
GOOD FRIDAY	MAR 29
EASTER SUNDAY & DAYLIGHT SAVING TIME STARTS	MAR 31
EASTER MONDAY	APR 1
PASSOVER BEGINS	APR 22
ST. GEORGE'S DAY	APR 23
EARLY MAY BANK HOLIDAY	MAY 6
SPRING BANK HOLIDAY	MAY 27
FATHER'S DAY (UK)	JUN 16
ISLAMIC NEW YEAR BEGINS	JUL 6
PUBLIC HOLIDAY (NORTHERN IRELAND)	JUL 12
SUMMER BANK HOLIDAY (SCOTLAND)	AUG 5
SUMMER BANK HOLIDAY (ENG, NIR, WAL)	AUG 26
INTERNATIONAL DAY OF PEACE (UNITED NATIONS)	SEP 21
ROSH HASHANAH (JEWISH NEW YEAR) BEGINS	OCT 2
WORLD MENTAL HEALTH DAY	OCT 10
YOM KIPPUR BEGINS	OCT 11
DAYLIGHT SAVING TIME ENDS	OCT 27
HALLOWEEN	OCT 31
DIWALI	NOV 1
GUY FAWKES NIGHT	NOV 5
REMEMBRANCE SUNDAY	NOV 10
ST. ANDREW'S DAY	NOV 30
CHRISTMAS DAY	DEC 25
BOXING DAY	DEC 26
NEW YEAR'S EVE	DEC 31

PLANNER 2024

JANUARY	FEBRUARY	MARCH
1 M	1 T	1 F
2 T	2 F	2 S
3 W	3 S	3 S
4 T	4 S	4 M
5 F	5 M	5 T
6 S	6 T	6 W
7 S	7 W	7 T
8 M	8 T	8 F
9 T	9 F	9 S
10 W	10 S	10 S
11 T	11 S	11 M
12 F	12 M	12 T
13 S	13 T	13 W
14 S	14 W	14 T
15 M	15 T	15 F
16 T	16 F	16 S
17 W	17 S	17 S
18 T	18 S	18 M
19 F	19 M	19 T
20 S	20 T	20 W
21 S	21 W	21 T
22 M	22 T	22 F
23 T	23 F	23 S
24 W	24 S	24 S
25 T	25 S	25 M
26 F	26 M	26 T
27 S	27 T	27 W
28 S	28 W	28 T
29 M	29 T	29 F
30 T		30 S
31 W		31 S

APRIL		MAY		JUNE	
1 M		1 W		1 S	
2 T		2 T		2 S	
3 W		3 F		3 M	
4 T		4 S		4 T	
5 F		5 S		5 W	
6 S		6 M		6 T	
7 S		7 T		7 F	
8 M		8 W		8 S	
9 T		9 T		9 S	
10 W		10 F		10 M	
11 T		11 S		11 T	
12 F		12 S		12 W	
13 S		13 M		13 T	
14 S		14 T		14 F	
15 M		15 W		15 S	
16 T		16 T		16 S	
17 W		17 F		17 M	
18 T		18 S		18 T	
19 F		19 S		19 W	
20 S		20 M		20 T	
21 S		21 T		21 F	
22 M		22 W		22 S	
23 T		23 T		23 S	
24 W		24 F		24 M	
25 T		25 S		25 T	
26 F		26 S		26 W	
27 S		27 M		27 T	
28 S		28 T		28 F	
29 M		29 W		29 S	
30 T		30 T		30 S	
		31 F			

JULY		AUGUST		SEPTEMBER	
1	M	1	T	1	S
2	T	2	F	2	M
3	W	3	S	3	T
4	T	4	S	4	W
5	F	5	M	5	T
6	S	6	T	6	F
7	S	7	W	7	S
8	M	8	T	8	S
9	T	9	F	9	M
10	W	10	S	10	T
11	T	11	S	11	W
12	F	12	M	12	T
13	S	13	T	13	F
14	S	14	W	14	S
15	M	15	T	15	S
16	T	16	F	16	M
17	W	17	S	17	T
18	T	18	S	18	W
19	F	19	M	19	T
20	S	20	T	20	F
21	S	21	W	21	S
22	M	22	T	22	S
23	T	23	F	23	M
24	W	24	S	24	T
25	T	25	S	25	W
26	F	26	M	26	T
27	S	27	T	27	F
28	S	28	W	28	S
29	M	29	T	29	S
30	T	30	F	30	M
31	W	31	S		

OCTOBER	NOVEMBER	DECEMBER
1 T	1 F	1 S
2 W	2 S	2 M
3 T	3 S	3 T
4 F	4 M	4 W
5 S	5 T	5 T
6 S	6 W	6 F
7 M	7 T	7 S
8 T	8 F	8 S
9 W	9 S	9 M
10 T	10 S	10 T
11 F	11 M	11 W
12 S	12 T	12 T
13 S	13 W	13 F
14 M	14 T	14 S
15 T	15 F	15 S
16 W	16 S	16 M
17 T	17 S	17 T
18 F	18 M	18 W
19 S	19 T	19 T
20 S	20 W	20 F
21 M	21 T	21 S
22 T	22 F	22 S
23 W	23 S	23 M
24 T	24 S	24 T
25 F	25 M	25 W
26 S	26 T	26 T
27 S	27 W	27 F
28 M	28 T	28 S
29 T	29 F	29 S
30 W	30 S	30 M
31 T		31 T

"Isn't it wonderful?"

Goals:

_____
_____
_____
_____
_____
_____
_____

To do:

_____
_____
_____
_____
_____
_____
_____

Birthdays:

_____
_____
_____
_____
_____
_____
_____
_____

1 MONDAY New Year's Day

2 TUESDAY New Year Holiday (Scotland)

3 WEDNESDAY

4 THURSDAY

FRIDAY 5

J

SATURDAY 6

SUNDAY 7

notes

8   MONDAY

9   TUESDAY

10   WEDNESDAY

11   THURSDAY

FRIDAY 12

SATURDAY 13

SUNDAY 14

notes

M T W T F S S M T W T F S S M T W T F S S M T W T F S S M T W
1 2 3 4 5 6 7 8 9 10 11 12 13 14 15 16 17 18 19 20 21 22 23 24 25 26 27 28 29 30 31

15 MONDAY

16 TUESDAY

17 WEDNESDAY

18 THURSDAY

FRIDAY 19

SATURDAY 20

SUNDAY 21

notes

22 MONDAY

23 TUESDAY

24 WEDNESDAY

25 THURSDAY

FRIDAY **26**

J

SATURDAY **27**

SUNDAY **28**

notes

M	T	W	T	F	S	S	M	T	W	T	F	S	S	M	T	W	T	F	S	S	M	T	W	T	F	S	S	M	T	W
1	2	3	4	5	6	7	8	9	10	11	12	13	14	15	16	17	18	19	20	21	22	23	24	25	26	27	28	29	30	31

FEBRUARY

Goals:
....
....
....
....
....
....
....

To do:
....
....
....
....
....
....

Birthdays:
....
....
....
....
....
....
....

29 MONDAY

30 TUESDAY

31 WEDNESDAY

1 THURSDAY

FRIDAY 2

SATURDAY 3

SUNDAY 4

notes

5 MONDAY

6 TUESDAY

7 WEDNESDAY

8 THURSDAY

FRIDAY 9

F

Chinese New Year (Dragon)

SATURDAY 10

SUNDAY 11

notes

T F S S M T W T F S S M T W T F S S M T W T F S S M T W T
1 2 3 4 5 6 7 8 9 10 11 12 13 14 15 16 17 18 19 20 21 22 23 24 25 26 27 28 29

12 MONDAY

13 TUESDAY

Shrove Tuesday

14 WEDNESDAY

Valentine's Day

15 THURSDAY

FRIDAY 16

SATURDAY 17

SUNDAY 18

notes

19 MONDAY

20 TUESDAY

21 WEDNESDAY

22 THURSDAY

FRIDAY 23

....
....
....
....
....
....
....

SATURDAY 24

....
....
....
....
....
....
....
....
....

SUNDAY 25

....
....
....
....
....

notes

....
....
....
....

T F S S M T W T F S S M T W T F S S M T W T F S S M T W T
1 2 3 4 5 6 7 8 9 10 11 12 13 14 15 16 17 18 19 20 21 22 23 24 25 26 27 28 29

"Full of Spirit"

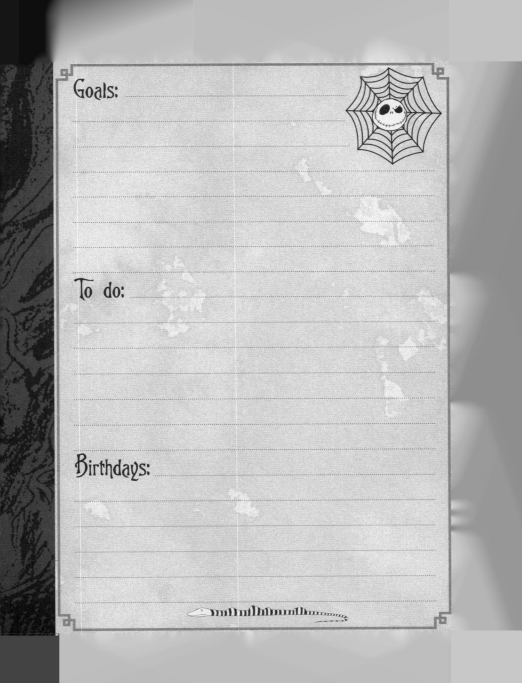

Goals:

....

....

....

....

....

....

....

To do:

....

....

....

....

....

....

Birthdays:

....

....

....

....

....

....

FEBRUARY 2024

26 MONDAY

27 TUESDAY

28 WEDNESDAY

29 THURSDAY

St. David's Day

FRIDAY 1

SATURDAY 2

SUNDAY 3

notes

T F S S M T W T F S S M T W T F S S M T W T F S S M T W T F S
15 16 17 18 19 20 21 22 23 24 25 26 27 28 29 | 1 2 3 4 5 6 7 8 9 10 11 12 13 14 15 16

MARCH 2024

4   MONDAY

5   TUESDAY

6   WEDNESDAY

7   THURSDAY

International Women's Day

FRIDAY 8

SATURDAY 9

Mother's Day (UK) & Ramadan Begins

SUNDAY 10

notes

F S S M T W T F S S M T W T F S S M T W T F S S M T W T F S S
1 2 3 4 5 6 7 8 9 10 11 12 13 14 15 16 17 18 19 20 21 22 23 24 25 26 27 28 29 30 31

11 MONDAY

12 TUESDAY

13 WEDNESDAY

14 THURSDAY

FRIDAY 15

SATURDAY 16

St. Patrick's Day

SUNDAY 17

ZERO

notes

F S S M T W T F S S M T W T F S S M T W T F S S M T W T F S S
1 2 3 4 5 6 7 8 9 10 11 12 13 14 15 16 17 18 19 20 21 22 23 24 25 26 27 28 29 30 31

18 MONDAY

19 TUESDAY

20 WEDNESDAY

21 THURSDAY

FRIDAY 22

SATURDAY 23

SUNDAY 24

notes

25 MONDAY

26 TUESDAY

27 WEDNESDAY

28 THURSDAY

FRIDAY 29

Good Friday

....

....

....

....

....

....

....

SATURDAY 30

....

....

....

....

....

....

....

Easter Sunday & Daylight Saving Time Starts

SUNDAY 31

....

....

....

....

....

notes

....

....

....

F S S M T W T F S S M T W T F S S M T W T F S S M T W T F S S
1 2 3 4 5 6 7 8 9 10 11 12 13 14 15 16 17 18 19 20 21 22 23 24 25 26 27 28 29 30 31

Goals:

....

....

....

....

....

....

....

To do:

....

....

....

....

....

....

Birthdays:

....

....

....

....

....

....

APRIL 2024

1 MONDAY

2 TUESDAY

3 WEDNESDAY

4 THURSDAY

FRIDAY 5

SATURDAY 6

SUNDAY 7

notes

M T W T F S S M T W T F S S M T W T F S S M T W T F S S M T
1 2 3 4 5 6 7 8 9 10 11 12 13 14 15 16 17 18 19 20 21 22 23 24 25 26 27 28 29 30

8 MONDAY

9 TUESDAY

10 WEDNESDAY

11 THURSDAY

FRIDAY 12

SATURDAY 13

SUNDAY 14

notes

M T W T F S S M T W T F S S M T W T F S S M T W T F S S M T
1 2 3 4 5 6 7 8 9 10 11 12 13 14 15 16 17 18 19 20 21 22 23 24 25 26 27 28 29 30

15 MONDAY

....

....

....

....

....

....

16 TUESDAY

....

....

....

....

....

....

17 WEDNESDAY

....

....

....

....

....

....

18 THURSDAY

....

....

....

....

....

FRIDAY 19

SATURDAY 20

SUNDAY 21

notes

M T W T F S S M T W T F S S M T W T F S S M T W T F S S M T
1 2 3 4 5 6 7 8 9 10 11 12 13 14 15 16 17 18 19 20 21 22 23 24 25 26 27 28 29 30

22 MONDAY

Passover Begins

23 TUESDAY

St. George's Day

24 WEDNESDAY

25 THURSDAY

FRIDAY 26

SATURDAY 27

A

SUNDAY 28

notes

MAY

Goals:
....
....
....
....
....
....

To do:
....
....
....
....
....

Birthdays:
....
....
....
....
....

29 MONDAY

30 TUESDAY

1 WEDNESDAY

2 THURSDAY

FRIDAY 3

SATURDAY 4

SUNDAY 5

notes

T W T F S S M T W T F S S M T W T F S S M T W T F S S M T W T
16 17 18 19 20 21 22 23 24 25 26 27 28 29 30 | 1 2 3 4 5 6 7 8 9 10 11 12 13 14 15 16

MAY 2024

6 MONDAY

Early May Bank Holiday

7 TUESDAY

8 WEDNESDAY

9 THURSDAY

FRIDAY 10

SATURDAY 11

M

SUNDAY 12

notes

W T F S S M T W T F S S M T W T F S S M T W T F S S M T W T F
1 2 3 4 5 6 7 8 9 10 11 12 13 14 15 16 17 18 19 20 21 22 23 24 25 26 27 28 29 30 31

13 MONDAY

---

14 TUESDAY

---

15 WEDNESDAY

---

16 THURSDAY

FRIDAY 17

SATURDAY 18

M

SUNDAY 19

notes

MAY 2024

20 MONDAY

21 TUESDAY

22 WEDNESDAY

23 THURSDAY

FRIDAY 24

SATURDAY 25

M

SUNDAY 26

notes

W T F S S M T W T F S S M T W T F S S M T W T F S S M T W T F
1 2 3 4 5 6 7 8 9 10 11 12 13 14 15 16 17 18 19 20 21 22 23 24 25 26 27 28 29 30 31

Goals:

_____
_____
_____
_____
_____
_____

To do:

_____
_____
_____
_____
_____
_____

Birthdays:

_____
_____
_____
_____
_____
_____

27 MONDAY

28 TUESDAY

29 WEDNESDAY

30 THURSDAY

FRIDAY 31

SATURDAY 1

SUNDAY 2

J

notes

3 MONDAY

4 TUESDAY

5 WEDNESDAY

6 THURSDAY

FRIDAY 7

SATURDAY 8

SUNDAY 9

notes

10 MONDAY

11 TUESDAY

12 WEDNESDAY

13 THURSDAY

FRIDAY 14

SATURDAY 15

Father's Day (UK)   SUNDAY 16

notes

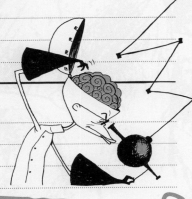

S S M T W T F S S M T W T F S S M T W T F S S M T W T F S S
1 2 3 4 5 6 7 8 9 10 11 12 13 14 15 16 17 18 19 20 21 22 23 24 25 26 27 28 29 30

JUNE 2024

17 MONDAY

18 TUESDAY

19 WEDNESDAY

20 THURSDAY

FRIDAY 21

SATURDAY 22

SUNDAY 23

notes

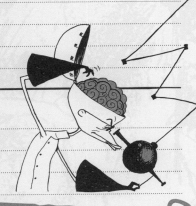

24 MONDAY

25 TUESDAY

26 WEDNESDAY

27 THURSDAY

FRIDAY 28

SATURDAY 29

SUNDAY 30

notes

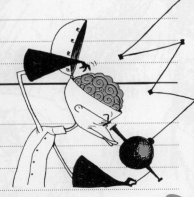

S	S	M	T	W	T	F	S	S	M	T	W	T	F	S	S	M	T	W	T	F	S	S	M	T	W	T	F	S	S
1	2	3	4	5	6	7	8	9	10	11	12	13	14	15	16	17	18	19	20	21	22	23	24	25	26	27	28	29	30

Goals:

To do:

Birthdays:

1 MONDAY

2 TUESDAY

3 WEDNESDAY

4 THURSDAY

FRIDAY 5

SATURDAY 6

Islamic New Year Begins

SUNDAY 7

notes

8 MONDAY

9 TUESDAY

10 WEDNESDAY

11 THURSDAY

Public Holiday (Northern Ireland)

FRIDAY 12

SATURDAY 13

SUNDAY 14

otes

M T W T F S S M T W T F S S M T W T F S S M T W T F S S M T W
1 2 3 4 5 6 7 8 9 10 11 12 13 14 15 16 17 18 19 20 21 22 23 24 25 26 27 28 29 30 31

15 MONDAY

16 TUESDAY

17 WEDNESDAY

18 THURSDAY

FRIDAY 19

....
....
....
....
....
....

....

SATURDAY 20

....
....
....

SUNDAY 21

....
....
....
....
....

notes

....
....
....
....

M T W T F S S M T W T F S S M T W T F S S M T W T F S S M T W
1 2 3 4 5 6 7 8 9 10 11 12 13 14 15 16 17 18 19 20 21 22 23 24 25 26 27 28 29 30 31

22 MONDAY

23 TUESDAY

24 WEDNESDAY

25 THURSDAY

FRIDAY 26

SATURDAY 27

J

SUNDAY 28

notes

M T W T F S S M T W T F S S M T W T F S S M T W T F S S M T W
1 2 3 4 5 6 7 8 9 10 11 12 13 14 15 16 17 18 19 20 21 22 23 24 25 26 27 28 29 30 31

AUGUST

Goals:
....
....
....
....
....

To do:
....
....
....
....
....

Birthdays:
....
....
....
....
....

29 MONDAY

30 TUESDAY

31 WEDNESDAY

1 THURSDAY

FRIDAY 2

SATURDAY 3

SUNDAY 4

notes

5 MONDAY

Summer Bank Holiday (Scotland)

6 TUESDAY

7 WEDNESDAY

8 THURSDAY

FRIDAY 9

SATURDAY 10

SUNDAY 11

A

notes

T F S S M T W T F S S M T W T F S S M T W T F S S M T W T F S
1 2 3 4 5 6 7 8 9 10 11 12 13 14 15 16 17 18 19 20 21 22 23 24 25 26 27 28 29 30 31

12 MONDAY

13 TUESDAY

14 WEDNESDAY

15 THURSDAY

FRIDAY 16

SATURDAY 17

SUNDAY 18

A

notes

T F S S M T W T F S S M T W T F S S M T W T F S S M T W T F S
1 2 3 4 5 6 7 8 9 10 11 12 13 14 15 16 17 18 19 20 21 22 23 24 25 26 27 28 29 30 31

19 MONDAY

20 TUESDAY

21 WEDNESDAY

22 THURSDAY

FRIDAY 23

SATURDAY 24

SUNDAY 25

A

notes

T F S S M T W T F S S M T W T F S S M T W T F S S M T W T F S
1 2 3 4 5 6 7 8 9 10 11 12 13 14 15 16 17 18 19 20 21 22 23 24 25 26 27 28 29 30 31

"I might Split a Seam"

Goals:

To do:

Birthdays:

26 MONDAY

27 TUESDAY

28 WEDNESDAY

29 THURSDAY

FRIDAY 30

SATURDAY 31

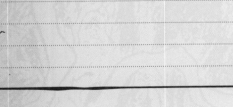

SUNDAY 1

8

notes

2 MONDAY

....
....
....
....
....
....

3 TUESDAY

....
....
....
....
....
....

4 WEDNESDAY

....
....
....
....
....
....

5 THURSDAY

....
....
....
....
....

FRIDAY 6

SATURDAY 7

SUNDAY 8

notes

9 MONDAY

10 TUESDAY

11 WEDNESDAY

12 THURSDAY

FRIDAY 13

SATURDAY 14

SUNDAY 15

8

notes

S M T W T F S S M T W T F S S M T W T F S S M T W T F S S M
1 2 3 4 5 6 7 8 9 10 11 12 13 14 15 16 17 18 19 20 21 22 23 24 25 26 27 28 29 30

16 MONDAY

17 TUESDAY

18 WEDNESDAY

19 THURSDAY

FRIDAY 20

International Day of Peace (United Nations)

SATURDAY 21

SUNDAY 22

notes

23 MONDAY

24 TUESDAY

25 WEDNESDAY

26 THURSDAY

FRIDAY 27

SATURDAY 28

SUNDAY 29

notes

"Creation of Dr. Finkelstein"

Goals:

....
....
....
....
....
....
....

To do:

....
....
....
....
....
....

Birthdays:

....
....
....
....
....
....

30 MONDAY

1 TUESDAY

2 WEDNESDAY

Rosh Hashanah (Jewish New Year) Begins

3 THURSDAY

FRIDAY 4

SATURDAY 5

SUNDAY 6

notes

7 MONDAY

8 TUESDAY

9 WEDNESDAY

10 THURSDAY

World Mental Health Day

FRIDAY 11

Yom Kippur Begins

SATURDAY 12

SUNDAY 13

notes

T W T F S S M T W T F S S M T W T F S S M T W T F S S M T W T
1 2 3 4 5 6 7 8 9 10 11 12 13 14 15 16 17 18 19 20 21 22 23 24 25 26 27 28 29 30 31

14 MONDAY

15 TUESDAY

16 WEDNESDAY

17 THURSDAY

FRIDAY 18

SATURDAY 19

SUNDAY 20

0

notes

T W T F S S M T W T F S S M T W T F S S M T W T F S S M T W T
1 2 3 4 5 6 7 8 9 10 11 12 13 14 15 16 17 18 19 20 21 22 23 24 25 26 27 28 29 30 31

21 MONDAY

22 TUESDAY

23 WEDNESDAY

24 THURSDAY

FRIDAY 25

SATURDAY 26

SUNDAY 27

Daylight Saving Time Ends

0

notes

T W T F S S M T W T F S S M T W T F S S M T W T F S S M T W T
1 2 3 4 5 6 7 8 9 10 11 12 13 14 15 16 17 18 19 20 21 22 23 24 25 26 27 28 29 30 31

Goals:
....
....
....
....
....
....
....

To do:
....
....
....
....
....

Birthdays:
....
....
....
....
....
....

28 MONDAY

29 TUESDAY

30 WEDNESDAY

31 THURSDAY

Halloween

FRIDAY 1

Diwali

SATURDAY 2

SUNDAY 3

notes

W	T	F	S	S	M	T	W	T	F	S	S	M	T	W	T	F	S	S	M	T	W	T	F	S	S	M	T	W	T	F
16	17	18	19	20	21	22	23	24	25	26	27	28	29	30	31	1	2	3	4	5	6	7	8	9	10	11	12	13	14	15

4 MONDAY

---

5 TUESDAY   Guy Fawkes Night

---

6 WEDNESDAY

---

7 THURSDAY

FRIDAY 8

SATURDAY 9

Remembrance Sunday

SUNDAY 10

notes

11 MONDAY

12 TUESDAY

13 WEDNESDAY

14 THURSDAY

FRIDAY 15

SATURDAY 16

SUNDAY 17

notes

F S S M T W T F S S M T W T F S S M T W T F S S M T W T F S
1 2 3 4 5 6 7 8 9 10 11 12 13 14 15 16 17 18 19 20 21 22 23 24 25 26 27 28 29 30

18 MONDAY

19 TUESDAY

20 WEDNESDAY

21 THURSDAY

FRIDAY 22

SATURDAY 23

SUNDAY 24

notes

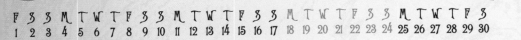

"No Sleep 'till Xmas"

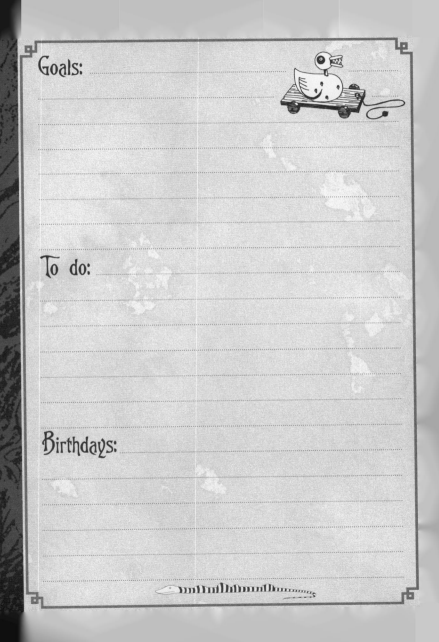

Goals:

To do:

Birthdays:

25 MONDAY

26 TUESDAY

27 WEDNESDAY

28 THURSDAY

FRIDAY 29

St. Andrew's Day

SATURDAY 30

SUNDAY 1

notes

S	S	M	T	W	T	F	S	S	M	T	W	T	F	S	S	M	T	W	T	F	S	S	M	T	W	T	F	S	S
16	17	18	19	20	21	22	23	24	25	26	27	28	29	30	1	2	3	4	5	6	7	8	9	10	11	12	13	14	15

D

2   MONDAY

3   TUESDAY

4   WEDNESDAY

5   THURSDAY

FRIDAY 6

SATURDAY 7

SUNDAY 8

notes

D

S	M	T	W	T	F	S	S	M	T	W	T	F	S	S	M	T	W	T	F	S	S	M	T	W	T	F	S	S	M	T
1	2	3	4	5	6	7	8	9	10	11	12	13	14	15	16	17	18	19	20	21	22	23	24	25	26	27	28	29	30	31

9 MONDAY

10 TUESDAY

11 WEDNESDAY

12 THURSDAY

DECEMBER 2024

FRIDAY 13

SATURDAY 14

SUNDAY 15

notes

D

16 MONDAY

17 TUESDAY

18 WEDNESDAY

19 THURSDAY

DECEMBER 2024

FRIDAY 20

SATURDAY 21

SUNDAY 22

notes

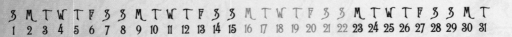

D

23 MONDAY

24 TUESDAY

25 WEDNESDAY

Christmas Day

26 THURSDAY

Boxing Day

FRIDAY 27

SATURDAY 28

SUNDAY 29

notes

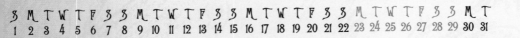

S M T W T F S S M T W T F S S M T W T F S S M T W T F S S M T
1 2 3 4 5 6 7 8 9 10 11 12 13 14 15 16 17 18 19 20 21 22 23 24 25 26 27 28 29 30 31

30 MONDAY

31 TUESDAY

New Year's Eve

1 WEDNESDAY

New Year's Day

2 THURSDAY

New Year Holiday (Scotland)

FRIDAY 3

SATURDAY 4

SUNDAY 5

notes

M T W T F S S M T W T F S S M | T W T F S S M T W T S S M T W T
16 17 18 19 20 21 22 23 24 25 26 27 28 29 30 31 | 1 2 3 4 5 6 7 8 9 10 11 12 13 14 15

J

PLANNER 2025

JANUARY		FEBRUARY		MARCH	
1	W	1	S	1	S
2	T	2	S	2	S
3	F	3	M	3	M
4	S	4	T	4	T
5	S	5	W	5	W
6	M	6	T	6	T
7	T	7	F	7	F
8	W	8	S	8	S
9	T	9	S	9	S
10	F	10	M	10	M
11	S	11	T	11	T
12	S	12	W	12	W
13	M	13	T	13	T
14	T	14	F	14	F
15	W	15	S	15	S
16	T	16	S	16	S
17	F	17	M	17	M
18	S	18	T	18	T
19	S	19	W	19	W
20	M	20	T	20	T
21	T	21	F	21	F
22	W	22	S	22	S
23	T	23	S	23	S
24	F	24	M	24	M
25	S	25	T	25	T
26	S	26	W	26	W
27	M	27	T	27	T
28	T	28	F	28	F
29	W			29	S
30	T			30	S
31	F			31	M

APRIL		MAY		JUNE	
1 T		1 T		1 S	
2 W		2 F		2 M	
3 T		3 S		3 T	
4 F		4 S		4 W	
5 S		5 M		5 T	
6 S		6 T		6 F	
7 M		7 W		7 S	
8 T		8 T		8 S	
9 W		9 F		9 M	
10 T		10 S		10 T	
11 F		11 S		11 W	
12 S		12 M		12 T	
13 S		13 T		13 F	
14 M		14 W		14 S	
15 T		15 T		15 S	
16 W		16 F		16 M	
17 T		17 S		17 T	
18 F		18 S		18 W	
19 S		19 M		19 T	
20 S		20 T		20 F	
21 M		21 W		21 S	
22 T		22 T		22 S	
23 W		23 F		23 M	
24 T		24 S		24 T	
25 F		25 S		25 W	
26 S		26 M		26 T	
27 S		27 T		27 F	
28 M		28 W		28 S	
29 T		29 T		29 S	
30 W		30 F		30 M	
		31 S			

PLANNER 2025

JULY	AUGUST	SEPTEMBER
1 T	1 F	1 M
2 W	2 S	2 T
3 T	3 S	3 W
4 F	4 M	4 T
5 S	5 T	5 F
6 S	6 W	6 S
7 M	7 T	7 S
8 T	8 F	8 M
9 W	9 S	9 T
10 T	10 S	10 W
11 F	11 M	11 T
12 S	12 T	12 F
13 S	13 W	13 S
14 M	14 T	14 S
15 T	15 F	15 M
16 W	16 S	16 T
17 T	17 S	17 W
18 F	18 M	18 T
19 S	19 T	19 F
20 S	20 W	20 S
21 M	21 T	21 S
22 T	22 F	22 M
23 W	23 S	23 T
24 T	24 S	24 W
25 F	25 M	25 T
26 S	26 T	26 F
27 S	27 W	27 S
28 M	28 T	28 S
29 T	29 F	29 M
30 W	30 S	30 T
31 T	31 S	

OCTOBER

1	W
2	T
3	F
4	S
5	S
6	M
7	T
8	W
9	T
10	F
11	S
12	S
13	M
14	T
15	W
16	T
17	F
18	S
19	S
20	M
21	T
22	W
23	T
24	F
25	S
26	S
27	M
28	T
29	W
30	T
31	F

NOVEMBER

1	S
2	S
3	M
4	T
5	W
6	T
7	F
8	S
9	S
10	M
11	T
12	W
13	T
14	F
15	S
16	S
17	M
18	T
19	W
20	T
21	F
22	S
23	S
24	M
25	T
26	W
27	T
28	F
29	S
30	S

DECEMBER

1	M
2	T
3	W
4	T
5	F
6	S
7	S
8	M
9	T
10	W
11	T
12	F
13	S
14	S
15	M
16	T
17	W
18	T
19	F
20	S
21	S
22	M
23	T
24	W
25	T
26	F
27	S
28	S
29	M
30	T
31	W

ADDRESS / PHONE NUMBERS

NAME

ADDRESS

TELEPHONE   MOBILE

EMAIL

NAME

ADDRESS

TELEPHONE   MOBILE

EMAIL

NAME

ADDRESS

TELEPHONE   MOBILE

EMAIL

NAME

ADDRESS

TELEPHONE   MOBILE

EMAIL

NAME

ADDRESS

TELEPHONE   MOBILE

EMAIL

NAME

ADDRESS

TELEPHONE   MOBILE

EMAIL

ADDRESS / PHONE NUMBERS

NAME

ADDRESS

TELEPHONE   MOBILE

EMAIL

NAME

ADDRESS

TELEPHONE   MOBILE

EMAIL

NAME

ADDRESS

TELEPHONE   MOBILE

EMAIL

NAME

ADDRESS

TELEPHONE   MOBILE

EMAIL

NAME

ADDRESS

TELEPHONE   MOBILE

EMAIL

NAME

ADDRESS

TELEPHONE   MOBILE

EMAIL

NOTES

NOTES